T0365808

Awareness Month Activity Book

Kevin Schoof

Copyright © 2015 Kevin Schoof.

All rights reserved. No part of this book may be used or reproduced by any means, graphic, electronic, or mechanical, including photocopying, recording, taping or by any information storage retrieval system without the written permission of the publisher except in the case of brief quotations embodied in critical articles and reviews.

WestBow Press books may be ordered through booksellers or by contacting:

WestBow Press
A Division of Thomas Nelson & Zondervan
1663 Liberty Drive
Bloomington, IN 47403
www.westbowpress.com
1 (866) 928-1240

Because of the dynamic nature of the Internet, any web addresses or links contained in this book may have changed since publication and may no longer be valid. The views expressed in this work are solely those of the author and do not necessarily reflect the views of the publisher, and the publisher hereby disclaims any responsibility for them.

Any people depicted in stock imagery provided by Thinkstock are models, and such images are being used for illustrative purposes only.
Certain stock imagery © Thinkstock.

ISBN: 978-1-4908-6604-8 (sc)
ISBN: 978-1-4908-6605-5 (e)

Library of Congress Control Number: 2015900458

Print information available on the last page.

WestBow Press rev. date: 3/6/2015

WESTBOW
PRESS
A DIVISION OF THOMAS NELSON
& ZONDERVAN

THIS BOOK'S INSPIRED BY A SPECIAL YOUNG MAN WITH AUTISM.

JANUARY THRU DECEMBER
THESE MONTHS ARE SPECIAL
TO REMEMBER. FOR A PET,
ADULT, TEEN, AND CHILD, WE
WANNA SEE EVERYBODY
SMILE. WE'RE ALL SPECIAL
IN GOD'S SIGHT, YELLOW, RED,
BLUE, BROWN, **BLACK**, GREEN,
PURPLE, OR WHITE.
THIS BOOK WAS MADE WITH
LOVE, SO GIVE YOURSELF A HUG!

JANUARY

("Count the Snowmen")

"Let's play in the snow and build snowmen with some friends!"

January Awareness

Birth Defects - Light Blue & Pink

Glaucoma - Green

Graves Disease - Light Blue

March of Dimes - Light Blue & Pink

Thyroid Disease - Light Blue

JANUARY

Find your way out of the maze and start celebrating the New Year!

FEBRUARY

("Count the Valentines")

"Make someone smile and give them a special valentine."

February Awareness

Anorexia Nervosa - Periwinkle

Bipolar Disorder - Green

Bulimia Nervosa - Periwinkle

Cardiovascular Disease - Red

Congenital Heart Defects - Red

Congenital Heart Disease - Red

Congestive Heart Failure - Red

Duchenne Muscular Dystrophy - Lime Green

Eating Disorders - Periwinkle

Heart Disease - Red

Macular Degeneration - Purple

Marfan Syndrome - Red

FEBRUARY

Cut out the valentine and give it to someone special!

To:

Be mine

From:

MARCH

("Count the Four-Leaf Clovers")

"Picking four-leaf clovers on a nice day can be a lot of fun."

March Awareness

Chronic Fatigue Syndrome - Dark Blue

Colon Cancer - Dark Blue

Colorectal Cancer - Dark Blue & Brown

Endometriosis - Yellow

Familial Polyposis - Brown

Hemophilia - Red

Kidney Cancer - Orange

Kidney Disease - Orange

Kidney Donation - Orange

Lymphedema - Dark Blue

Mental Retardation - Green

Multiple Sclerosis - Orange

Rectal Cancer - Dark Blue

Short Bowel Syndrome - Dark Blue

Spay or Neuter Pets - Dark Blue

MARCH

Connect the dots and have fun on St Patrick's Day!

APRIL

("Count the Easter Eggs")

"Finding colorful Easter eggs is a great way to spend the day."

April Awareness

Animal Abuse - Purple

Asperger Syndrome - Yellow, Red, Light Blue & Dark Blue

Autism - Yellow, Red, Light Blue & Dark Blue

Cesarean Section - Burgundy

Child Abuse Prevention - Dark Blue

Cushing Syndrome - Light Blue

Drug Abuse Resistance Education (DARE) - Red

Driving Under the Influence - Red

Environment - Green

Head and Neck Cancer - Red & White

Irritable Bowel Syndrome - Periwinkle

Living Organ Donation - Green

Mother's Against Drunken Drivers (MADD) - Red

Oral Cancer - Red & White

Organ Donation - Green

Organ Transplant - Green

Parkinson's Disease - Silver

Post-Traumatic Stress Disorder - Teal

Sarcoidosis - Purple

Sjogren's Syndrome - Purple

Substance Abuse - Red & Teal

Testicular Cancer - Purple

Tissue Donation - Green

APRIL

Match and color the pretty Easter eggs!

MAY

("Count the Baseballs")

"Nothing like playing a nice game of baseball in the park."

May Awareness

Addison's Disease - Light Blue

Allergies - Gray

Arthritis - Dark Blue

Asthma - Gray

Behcets Disease - Light Blue

Brain Cancer - Gray

Brain Tumor - Gray

Celiac Disease - Light Green

Cerebral Palsy - Green

Childhood Depression - Green

Colitis - Dark Blue

Crohn's Disease - Dark Blue

Cystic Fibrosis - Purple

Elderly Abuse - Silver

Fibromyalgia (men/women) - Purple

Food Allergies - Teal

Foster Care - Lavender

Gullian Barre Syndrome - Dark Blue

Hearing Disorders - Gold & Silver

Hearing Impairments - Gold & Silver

Hepatitis C - Red & Yellow

High Blood Pressure - Red

Huntington's Disease - Dark Blue

Lyme Disease - Lime Green

Lupus - Purple

ME/CFIDS - Dark Blue

Melanoma - Black & Orange

Mental Health - Green

Mental Illness - Green

Missing Children - Green

Muscular Dystrophy - Lime Green

Neurofibromatosis - Green

Pediatric Stroke - Purple & Blue

Pulmonary Arterial Hypertension - Purple

Rheumatoid Arthritis - Purple & Blue

Schizophrenia - Silver

Skin Cancer - Orange

Sleep Apnea - Black

Sleep Disorders - Black

Spinal Cord Injury - Green

Stroke - Red

Tinnitus - Gold & Silver

Tourette's Syndrome - Green

Troop Military Support - Yellow

MAY

Connect the dots and play baseball with your friends!

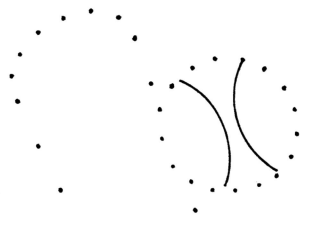

June Awareness

Antiphospholipid Antibody Syndrome - Burgundy

Aphasia - Gray

Headaches - Burgundy

Scleroderma - Teal

Tourette's Syndrome - Green

JUNE

Color the beautiful flowers found in a garden!

July Awareness

Sarcoma - Yellow

JULY

Find your way out of the maze and celebrate the 4th of July!

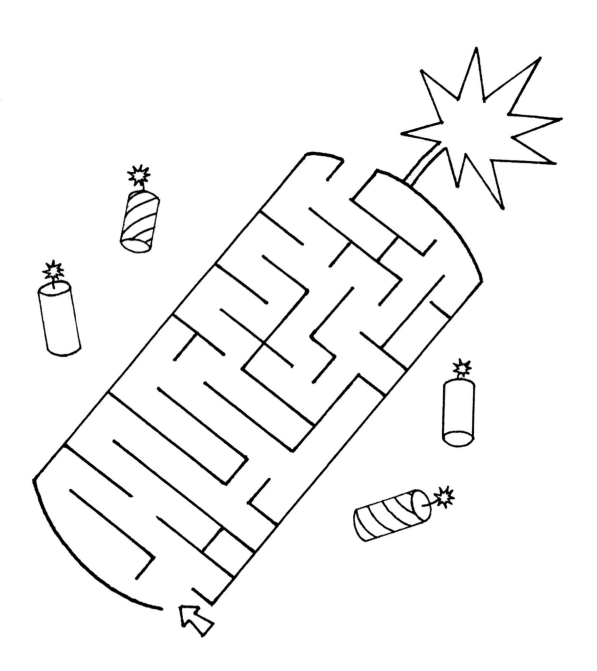

AUGUST

("Count the Seashells")

"Spending a summer day at the beach with friends is fun!"

August Awareness

Bone Cancer - White

Drowning - Dark Blue

Meningitis - Burgundy

Meningococcal Meningitis - Burgundy

Psoriasis - Orchid & Orange

Steven Johnson Syndrome - Dark Blue

Velo-Cardio Facial Syndrome - **Light Blue**

AUGUST

Match and color the seashells found on the beach!

SEPTEMBER

("Count the Balloons")

"What is your favorite animal at the zoo?"

September Awareness

9/11 - Red & White

ADHD - Purple

Adhesions - Burgundy

Alopecia - Dark Blue

Brain Aneurysm - Burgundy

Childhood Cancer - Gold

Chronic Illness - Light Blue

Dystonia - Dark Blue

Endometrial Cancer - Peach

Gynecological Cancer - Lavender

Hystiocytosis - Dark Blue

Leukemia - Orange

Leukodystrophies - Dark Blue

Liver Cancer - Yellow

Lymphoma - Lime Green

Mitochondrial Disease - Green

Myositis - Dark Blue

Non-Hodgkin's Lymphoma - Lime Green

Ovarian Cancer - Teal

Polycystic Ovarian Syndrome - Teal

Prostate Cancer - Light Blue

Reye's Syndrome - Dark Blue

Sickle Cell Anemia - Burgundy

Thyroid Cancer - Purple

Uterine Cancer - Peach

Victims of 9/11 WTC - Purple

WTC Heroes - Red & White

WTC Victims - Red & White

SEPTEMBER

Draw your favorite zoo animal!

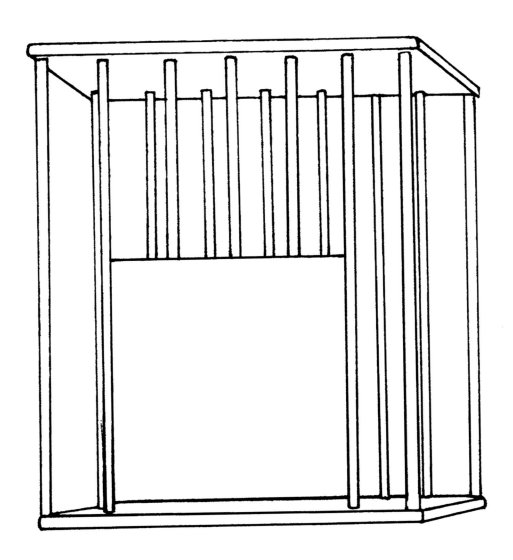

OCTOBER
("Count the Jack-O-Lanterns")

"What is your favorite Halloween costume?"

October Awareness

Anti-Bullying - Teal

Anxiety Disorder - Teal

Breast Cancer - Pink

Cultural Diversity - Orange

Depression - Green

Down Syndrome - Blue & Yellow

Dyslexia - Silver

Eczema - Orchid & Orange

Hunger - Orange

Interstitial Cystitis - Dark Blue

Literacy - Green

Manic Depression - Green

Mental Illness - Gray

Post-Polio Syndrome - Burgundy

Schizophrenia - Silver

Spina Bifida - Yellow

Sudden Infant Death Syndrome (SIDS) - Pink & Light Blue

Victim's Rights - Dark Blue

OCTOBER

Find your way out of the jack-o-lantern and go trick or treating!

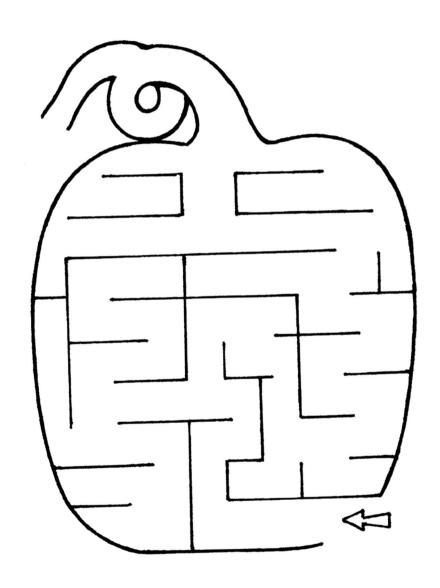

NOVEMBER

("Count the Turkeys")

"Jumping in big piles of leaves makes me laugh!"

November Awareness

Adoptee - White

Adoption - White

Alpha-1 Antitrypsin - Purple

Alzheimer's Disease - Purple

Anti-Tobacco - Brown

Bone Marrow Donation - Green

Caregiver - Lavender

Colitis - Purple

COPD - Gold

Crohn's Disease - Purple

Diabetes - Gray

Domestic Violence - Purple

Emphysema - Pearl

Epilepsy - Lavender

Homelessness - Purple

Hospice Care - Burgundy

Hypertension - Red

Juvenile Diabetes - Gray

Lung Cancer - Pearl

Lung Disease - Pearl

Pancreatic Cancer - Purple

Pancreatitis (Chronic) - Purple

Premature Birth - Pink & Light Blue

Pulmonary Hypertension - Periwinkle

RSD/CRPS - Orange

NOVEMBER

Connect the dots and celebrate Thanksgiving!

DECEMBER
("Count the Ornaments")

"Do you like to help decorate the Christmas tree?"

December Awareness

Aplastic Anemia - Red

Bone Marrow - Red

DECEMBER

Decorate the tree for a special Christmas celebration!

Printed in the United States
By Bookmasters